Old ROYAL DEESIDE

by

David Jamieson and W. Stewart Wilson

In early times the lands of Balmoral formed part of the Earldom of Mar, later becoming the property of a branch of the Farquharsons of Inverey. They remained in their possession until the middle of the eighteenth century when they were acquired by the Earl of Fife. In 1847 Queen Victoria and Prince Albert had a miserable, wet holiday at Ardverikie, Loch Laggan, and the Queen's doctor, Sir James Clark, persuaded them to try the drier climate of Deeside. Queen Victoria arrived on Deeside with the royal family in September 1848 and subsequently purchased the old castle and estate of Balmoral at a cost of £31,500. The existing castle was demolished and the present Balmoral built in its place. Its foundation stone was laid in 1853 and it was completed in 1855.

© David Jamieson and W. Stewart Wilson 2001
First published in the United Kingdom, 2001,
by Stenlake Publishing Ltd.
54-58 Mill Square, Catrine, KA5 6RD
01290 551122
www.stenlake.co.uk

ISBN 9781840331370

Printed by Blissetts, Roslin Road, Acton, W3 8DH

The publishers regret that they cannot supply
copies of any pictures featured in this book.

ACKNOWLEDGEMENTS

We would like to thank all those who have given of their local knowledge including Mrs Jean Bowman, Miss Sybil Innes, Dr Archie Milne, Mr Michael Robson, and Miss Marjorie H. Walker. Mr Sam McBrearty and Mrs Sheena L. Hepburn kindly lent postcards from their collections. We are also grateful to Robert Grieves who provided the pictures and accompanying captions on the inside front cover, page 36, page 44 and the inside back cover.

FURTHER READING

Many books have been written in praise of Royal Deeside. The authors have found the following selection of particular interest and recommend them to those who wish to explore the area further. They are listed in chronological order of original publication dates. None of them are available from Stenlake Publishing, and those interested in finding out more are advised to contact their local bookshop or reference library.

An Account of the Parish of Birse, Robert Dinnie, republished by Birse Community Trust, 1999.
Deeside, Alex McConnochie, republished by EP Publishing, 1972.
The Old Deeside Road, G. M. Fraser, republished by Robin Callander, 1980.
Royal Valley, Fenton Wyness, Alex P. Reid, 1968.
The Royal Deeside Line, A. D. Farr, David and Charles, 1968.
Stories of Royal Deeside's Railway, A. D. Farr, Kestrel Books, 1971.
Portrait of Aberdeen and Deeside, Cuthbert Graham, Robert Hale, 1972.
History in Birse Volumes 1–4, Robin Callander, republished by Birse Community Trust, 2000.
Royal Deeside, John S. Smith, Aberdeen University Library, 1984.
Valley of the Dee, Robert Smith, Aberdeen University Library, 1989.
Discovering Aberdeenshire, Robert Smith, John Donald, 1998.
Royal Deeside's Railway, Dick Jackson, Great North of Scotland Railway Association, 1999.
The Dee from the Far Grampians, Ian Murray, Lochnagar Publications, 1999.
Scenery of the Dee, Jim Henderson, Crooktree Images, 2000.
A Queen's Country, Robert Smith, John Donald, 2000.

INTRODUCTION

Our schooldays began with the three R's, and the towns and countryside of Upper Deeside can be introduced by referring to three other R's – River, Royalty and Relaxation – all of which characterise this beautiful part of north-east Scotland.

Deeside takes its name from the River Dee, which rises at a height of over 4,000 feet from the Wells of Dee near the summit of Braeriach amongst the Grampian Mountains. The river follows a course of over 85 miles before reaching the North Sea at Aberdeen, initially dropping 2,000 feet into Glen Dee where it becomes the fastest flowing river in Scotland. Over the years the river has been praised not only by anglers for its salmon and trout, but also by many writers who have celebrated it in verse and prose. 'On its sparkling waters not a single reach of its scenery lacks beauty or interest, while at many points its charms can hardly be surpassed' wrote Alex. McConnochie in 1893.

Along the length of its south bank the river is overlooked by the Mounth, from the Gaelic *monadh* meaning 'mountain' or 'moorland', which shuts off Deeside from the south. It is crossed by only nine passes, through which marauding armies have sought to invade the north and raiders and illicit whisky smugglers have crossed south to Angus and Perthshire. After Edward I crossed the Mounth on his path of conquest in the early fourteenth century the next royal visitor from England was Queen Victoria, who was herself conquered by the splendour of Deeside.

When the Queen arrived at Aberdeen on Friday 8 September 1848 she was the first member of the royal family to visit the city for centuries, and as she drove up the Deeside road to view the Balmoral estate her carriage passed under 23 triumphal arches. She quickly felt the relaxed spirit of the Highlands, remarking that 'All seemed to breathe freedom and peace and to make us forget the world and its turmoils.' When Robert Louis Stevenson was on holiday in Braemar in 1881 he wrote in a letter to a friend that 'The Queen knows a thing or two – she has picked out the finest habitable spot in Britain.'

Before the arrival of the Queen and all the subsequent publicity, Deeside had inspired local poets and writers, although the first tourist guide to the area, *A Guide to the Highlands of Deeside,* by James Brown, was only written in 1831. In 1869, three years after his death, it was discovered that the author had in fact been Joseph Robertson, who had written the guide at the age of 21 whilst on holiday in Ballater. He later became Curator of the Historical Department in Register House, Edinburgh. In his book he hinted that tourism was beginning to affect the area when he expressed his concern that Deeside was about to be 'desolated by cockneys and other horrid reptiles'!

By 1868, when Queen Victoria wrote about her 'dear Paradise' in her *Journal of our Life in the Highlands,* the tourists had well and truly arrived. The Deeside Railway from Aberdeen reached Banchory in September 1853 and was extended to Aboyne in December 1859 and Ballater in October 1866. Thus tourists, intrigued by the area's royal associations, were easily able to reach the valley from the coast. However, the proposed extension of the line to Braemar, past the Balmoral estate, was abandoned when Queen Victoria objected, 'wishing the upper part of the Dee Valley to be preserved as a natural Highland region'.

George Washington Wilson, Scotland's first Photographer Royal, was commissioned to photograph the rebuilding of Balmoral in 1854 by Prince Albert, and produced a book of photographic views of Aberdeen and Deeside in 1856. He was thus the first photographer to recognise the potential commercial value of the tourists, who were eager to buy picturesque views of the valley as mementos of their visits. Tourism continued to be encouraged throughout the latter half of the nineteenth century prompting Alex. McConnochie to write in 1900 that 'the summer visitors come in such numbers as almost to cancel out the permanent residents.'

Ever since, the villages and towns of Upper Deeside have expanded to meet the demands of visitors and tourists in the building of hotels, renting of houses and provision of shops. The various Highland Games are world famous and the roads, especially since the closure of the railway in 1966, have been improved. Despite its popularity, the Valley of the Dee still retains its attractiveness in every season of the year. The royal status of Deeside is as strong as ever and Queen Victoria's words of 1856 still remain true to the area today: 'I love my peaceful, wild Highlands, the glorious scenery, the dear good people who are much attached to us.'

On leaving Banchory there are three main routes to Aboyne. Having passed the Bridge of Feugh on the South Deeside Road, one reaches the village of Strachan (above) which derives its name from the stream which joins the River Feugh just west of the village – the Aven. This is known locally as the Aan, and the name of village is in turn pronounced 'Straan'. Strachan has been a place of some importance from an early date, as it stands at the crossing of the Feugh on the road leading from Deeside to the Cairn a' Mounth pass to the south. The parish church (right) was gifted by Lady Gladstone of Glendye Estate and dates from 1865. There are three artificial, circular mounds nearby which may have been used as fences for bowmen when practising archery. The farmhouse on the lower side of the church is called Bowbutts. Despite its small size, Strachan has produced several eminent citizens including Thomas Reid, founder of the Scottish or Common Sense school of philosophy.

The Mill of Clinter in the parish of Birse dates from the early 1800s and is still owned by the same family that worked it then, the Mortimers. Meal mills have operated on this site since the early sixteenth century and the Mortimer family have worked in Birse since at least the seventeenth century. The name Birse is derived from the Gaelic *preis* meaning a thicket. Although it no longer grinds, the mill machinery remains in place and is still used for bruising and riddling. Until relatively recently Clinter's meal was widely famed, and it is only during the last 40 years that the area has ceased to be an important centre for milling grain from all over the parish.

RIVER FEUGH AT MILL OF CLINTER

In the nineteenth century there were several sawmills in Birse – in particular the Upper and Lower Sawmills. The Lower Mill stood on the site of the present Finzean Sawmill (pictured here), which is operated by David Duncan, the fourth generation of his family to work there. The Upper Mill stood on the site now occupied by the Bucket Mill, where wooden pails are once again being manufactured. The river still provides the power for these mills and at one time was also used to generate electricity for lighting. Birse Community Trust, which was set up in 1999, is committed to ensuring the conservation and continued operation of Finzean's unique nineteenth century mills.

SAWMILL, FINZEAN

Birse Castle

Old Castle, Forest of Birse

Birse Castle, which occupies a commanding position at the head of the Feugh Valley guarding the ancient path from Aboyne to Glen Esk, was built about the middle of the sixteenth century by Sir Thomas Gordon of Cluny on lands formerly belonging to the Bishops of Aberdeen.

> High on the bonnie hills o' Birse,
> Stan's good Sir Thomas's tower,
> And far and wide the oak tree spreads
> That shades his lady's bower.

By the late eighteenth century it was at the centre of a thriving community, with illicit stills providing the main source of livelihood. For many years the castle stood in a ruinous state, but it was subsequently restored, as shown in the postcard view on the left (sent in 1907). Annie, Viscountess Cowdray, took a great interest in Birse Castle and her grandson Charles Pearson, brother of the 4th Lord Cowdray, is at present carrying out extensive refurbishment of the castle which is let to shooting parties.

The Right Hon. Dr Robert Farquharson (seated) was MP for West Aberdeenshire for 26 years and in 1918 was succeeded as laird by his brother Joseph Farquharson RA (standing to the left of his brother), who gained great fame as a landscape painter. He is particularly remembered for his local scenes, many of which included sheep and snow and earned him the nickname 'Frozen Mutton Farquharson'. The message on this postcard, dated 15 October 1906 and sent to the vet in Tarland, reads 'Patient died Saturday morning'.

FINZEAN HOUSE.

The lands of Finzean (pronounced Fing-an and meaning 'the fair place') were acquired by the Farquharson family in 1609. The original Finzean House was built in 1686 and in 1749 a south wing was added. Considerable alterations were again made in 1790 and about 1860 the three gables and main entrance door were added. In 1954 a disastrous fire destroyed part of the house but the rebuilt structure retains the traditional style of frontage.

James Greig took over the shop in Finzean in 1886 and continued to run it until his retirement in the late 1920s. This postcard, published by himself, shows him at his stand at the Green, Aberdeen. By the time he retired, Greig's business included a van that toured the vicinity and a petrol pump. James Greig was later chosen to be the spokesman at the presentation of the fountain erected in the memory of Joseph Farquharson, who died in 1935.

The Station, Glassel.

The route of the Deeside Railway from Banchory was forced to take a wide sweep to the north-west of the town when proposals were made to extend it along the River Dee, because several landowners objected to the line passing through their estates. Stations were built at Glassel, Torphins, Lumphanan, Dess and Aboyne (the terminus), with the extension opening for service in December 1859. Glassel station served the area's scattered community and must have given folk a very welcome alternative means of transport, offering them the possibility of work as far afield as Aberdeen. Freight services were withdrawn in June 1965 and passenger services ceased in February 1966. The station building remains, having been converted into a private residence.

The smiddy would have been one of the busiest places in any community a hundred years ago. It was there that the blacksmith shoed horses and the wheelwright expertly fashioned cartwheels. Glassel's old smiddy, which stands on the north side of the A980, immediately beyond the junction of the road from the station, is presently being converted into a private house.

Glassel's only shop supplied local folk with everything they needed. This scene, which dates from the early twentieth century, has changed little over the last hundred years. The shop is still in the same location and benefits from the caravan site which adjoins the property. You can still post a letter here, but the box is no longer set into the wall of the shop. Now that bicycles are no longer the principal means of transport, a garage adjoining the shop serves locals and tourists who take this road to Torphins and beyond.

Campfield Shop and House, Glassel

The fine old Ha' House (Hall House) of Craigmyle was demolished in 1960. It stood about two miles west of Glassel on the lower slopes of the Hill o' Fare, facing south-west. Built in 1676 by Isabel Burnett of Craigmyle and her husband John Farquharson of Invercauld, it was restored and added to at the beginning of the twentieth century from designs by Sir Robert Lorimer. For a few years prior to 1887 there was a private platform on the Deeside Railway for the use of the residents of the house and their visitors. In 1956 the ancient barony of Craigmyle was broken up and four years later the house was demolished.

THE SQUARE AND HOTEL, TORPHINS

98595

Torphins may have got its name from Thorfin, Jarl of Orkney and a cousin of King Duncan and Macbeth. Having defeated Duncan in battle on the Morayshire coast, Thorfin pursued the remnants of the king's army south and is said to have rested here before returning home to the Orkneys. The village first sprang to prominence in 1596 when 'Torfynnes' was mentioned repeatedly at the local witchcraft trials, the 'gryt stane' on Craiglash Hill where the witches foregathered being only a short distance from the village. With the coming of the railway in 1859, what was then a village of 'a few thackit cottages near an old wayside inn' grew in importance. Colonel Thomas Innes, 5th Laird of Learney, was quick to appreciate its potential and was the 'architect' of much of the present village. Torphins became a favourite holiday resort in the years preceding the First World War and the Learney Arms Hotel dates from that period.

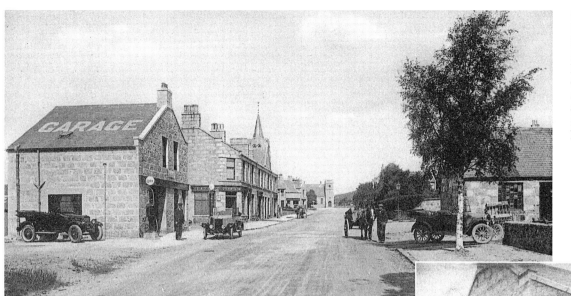

CRAIGOUR ROAD, TORPHINS.

Craigour Road with the Learney Hall in the far distance. The hall was built in 1899 and presented to the parish of Kincardine O'Neil by Lt. Col. F. N. Innes in commemoration of his parents' 60th wedding anniversary. Cars await attention outside the garage, while opposite a horse and cart approaches the smiddy's shop. Both garage and smiddy have now been replaced by housing.

In the early part of the twentieth century this shop on Craigour Road, Torphins, was owned by A. Hendry, tailor and clothier. At that time it was commonplace to visit a tailor, choose some cloth and be measured for a suit or outfit rather than to make do with something 'off the peg'. The message on this postcard, which dates from 1906 and was sent to a Miss Beveridge, reads: 'I will call tomorrow (Friday) at eleven o'clock to refit bodice and skirt and trust that will be suitable. Yours faithfully, A Hendry'. How was that for service!

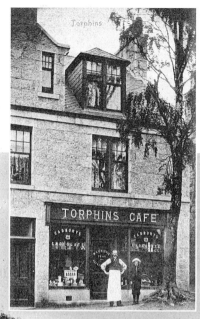

The fountain in The Square, Torphins, was erected by public subscription in 1897 to commemorate the 60th year of 'Queen Victoria's Beneficent Reign'. A thistle, rose, shamrock and fleur-de-lis (or could it be a leek?) are cut into the stone round the top of it. This picture was taken in the early part of the last century and the shops can be identified through a magnifying glass – from right to left they are a tobacconists with a sign above the door reading 'Smoke Mitchell's XXX Bogie Roll and Cut Golden Bar'; a cycle shop; Hector Taylor, chemist and druggist; W. Toller, shoemaker; Torphins Cafe (obscured by the fountain, but also shown in the smaller picture); A. Reid, saddler; and on the corner Alex. Williamson, general merchant. Four of the shops have now become private houses. The tobacconist's and cycle shop next door have been a butcher's since 1935 and the business has been owned by G. & D. Sinclair since 1972. The shop at the far corner is now occupied by a small supermarket.

This shop on Craigour Road, Torphins was occupied by Joseph Walker (shown here on the left), founder of the firm of the same name. In 1898 Joseph, then 21, opened a bakery with a loan of £50 and the dream of making the best shortbread in the world. Soon shooting parties from local estates were making detours to the bakery. As his fame spread and demand for his quality shortbread increased, Joseph took the first steps to expanding the business by moving to a larger shop in the Speyside village of Aberlour. The original shortbread recipe is still used today, and along with their range of cakes and biscuits Walker's shortbread can be found on sale in Harrods, as well as over 50 countries throughout the world . . . and it all began here in Torphins!

Lumphanan is a village of ancient origin and derives its name from the Welsh *llan*, meaning a church or enclosure, and Finnan, the name of the Welsh missionary and disciple of St Mungo who brought Christianity to these parts in the seventh century. The original village was known as Kirkton of Lumphanan and grew up around St Finnan's foundation. When the Deeside Railway arrived in 1859 the village station was erected half a mile to the east, prompting a new village to spring up around it. Dominating the scene and sitting on a high knoll backed by wooded slopes is the Stothart Memorial Church, erected in 1870, with its tower and lofty steeple. The train in the station is heading for Torphins.

Lumphanan from Golf Hill

MACBETH CAIRN, LUMPHANAN.

The story of Macbeth pervades this area – his death took place within the bounds of the parish and not at Dunsinane as related by Shakespeare. Near the church, which is about half a mile south-west of the village, is a spring called Macbeth's Well, and a quarter of a mile to the south of what is now the farm of Cairnbeathie is Macbeth's Stone, where tradition says the fugitive king was wounded in 1057. His enemies finally closed with him on Perkhill where he was killed in a hand-to-hand struggle with Macduff. His head was then cut off and carried to Malcolm Canmore, who had remained at Kincardine O'Neil. According to legend his body was buried under the cairn, known as Macbeth's Cairn, on the southern slopes of Perkhill (pictured here). In 1855 some bones were discovered within the cairn, but the grave chamber that was unearthed cannot have been Macbeth's as it is known that he was buried alongside the other Scottish kings on Iona. The memory of Macbeth is further perpetuated by the Macbeth Arms Hotel in Lumphanan.

Potarch Hotel.

Donald Dinnie started competing in the Aboyne Games from their revival in 1867, and although his records have now been broken few can rival his all-round achievement of 11,000 contests, 150 championships and £26,000 in prize money. This postcard is signed and dated April 1913, three years before Dinnie's death at the age of 78.

The main route from Banchory to Aboyne is by the North Deeside Road which travels along the north side of the Dee Valley and provides many fine views of the river. The Potarch Hotel lies to the south across the Bridge of Potarch. The original inn dates from around 1814 when the bridge was completed and the fairs that were formerly held at Marywell were moved to the Green, now a favourite spot for picnics. The inn was considerably enlarged in 1897. The Dinnie Stones, the famed training weights of Donald Dinnie, stand outside the hotel porch. These two stones with metal rings attached weigh a total of 785 lb. It is said that Dinnie's father used the stones as anchors while he was repairing the bridge, and that on completion of the work his son carried them across the bridge and continued to use them as training weights.

Regd. Copyright   Photo., G.L.C.

Donald Dinnie at 69

Thine truly
Donald Dinnie

It is claimed that Kincardine O'Neil is the oldest community on Deeside, and the village probably dates from the fifth century when it is mentioned in connection with St Erchard, a native of the parish who flourished at that time. The O'Neil portion of the name refers to the ancient Celtic thanage of Onele. The ruined kirk (left), dedicated to the Blessed Virgin, is a distinctive feature of the village which came into prominence during the thirteenth century, largely due to the influence of the powerful Durward family. It suffered greatly, however, when the Deeside Railway bypassed it by way of Torphins and Lumphanan. This picture shows the Neil Burn with the bridge over it lined by children from the local school. On the other side of the road is the present church, built in 1861 and opened the following year.

A battalion of the London Scottish march past the ivy-covered ruins of the kirk, which was established as a hospice and chapel circa 1240 by the Durwards. In time it became the parish church and served as such until its heather thatched roof caught fire in 1733. It was re-roofed and slated, but in 1859, the same year as the raising of the London Scottish as a volunteer force, it was declared unsafe. It is reported that the markets which were held at various times of the year in the village often encroached upon the kirkyard. A contemporary account describes the scene thus – 'Many hundreds of persons assemble themselves in the kirkyard with horses, creels and baggage of all kinds; some let their horses, several scores in number, run loose among the graves, and others tie them up by the sides of the church as to stalls; some erect tents and booths, while others expose their wares upon the graves of the dead, and in the very porch of the church.' In 1916 the London Scottish opted to become part of the Corps of the Gordon Highlanders and adopted the title in 1936 of The London Scottish (The Gordon Highlanders).

LONDON SCOTTISH". PASSING THE OLD CHURCH RUINS, KINCARDINE O' NEIL

Kincardine O'Neil became a burgh of barony in 1511 and as such would have had a barony inn, with the baron's armorial bearings displayed over the entrance. In order to ensure high standards, the inn would have been inspected regularly. The Gordon Arms has stood at this spot for nearly two hundred years and takes its name from Francis Gordon, the local laird, who purchased nearby Kincardine House about 1817.

Gordon Arms Hotel, Kincardine-O-Neil.

In 1233 a hospice (the first on Deeside) was established by Alan the Durward in Kincardine O'Neil. The village was also an important resting place for the drovers of old who used the ford which crossed the Dee below it. This can be approached by the road opposite the Gordon Arms and was much used prior to the building of the bridge at Potarch in 1814, providing a link with the south across the Cairn a' Mounth. The ford is sometimes referred to as Cochran's Ford. Cochran was a tenant crofter who is said to have provided lodgings for King James V when he paid a visit to the village in the sixteenth century. In return the king granted Cochran the gift of the croft, which still stands today on the eastern approach to the village. Kincardine House (pictured here) was rebuilt in the 1890s.

The village of Aboyne or Charleston of Aboyne owes its origins to Charles Gordon, 1st Earl of Aboyne, who obtained a charter granting him permission to erect a burgh of barony near the gates of his home, Aboyne Castle, in 1676. Like other burghs of barony Aboyne enjoyed certain privileges, such as the right to erect a tolbooth and a market cross, and to hold markets on the village green. The tolbooth and cross have long since disappeared, but the green still fronts the Huntly Arms Hotel. This takes its name from the Huntly title which came into the family of the Earls of Aboyne on the death of the 5th Duke of Gordon in 1836. To mark the new millennium, impressive gates have been erected at the main entrance to the green. In front of the gates stands the fountain which was erected by the inhabitants of Aboyne and neighbourhood to commemorate Queen Victoria's Diamond Jubilee in 1897 and the Coronation of King Edward VII in 1902.

SUSPENSION BRIDGE, ABOYNE FROM SOUTH 109

The original hamlet of Aboyne was called Bonty and stood next to the ford and ferry which provided a means of crossing the Dee. The site is marked by the Boat Inn, which was once a single thatched house with byre and stables. When the river was in spate in 1827 two people lost their lives making the ferry crossing, and this accident prompted the then Earl of Aboyne to set about constructing a suspension bridge across the Dee. Before it was completed, however, the 'Muckle Spate' of August 1829 swept away the partly-built bridge and its scaffolding. Another bridge was designed and was completed in 1831. It proved inadequate for heavy traffic, and in 1871 a third suspension bridge (above) was erected on the spot. Some of the materials from the earlier bridge were incorporated into the new structure, including the Marquis of Huntly's coat of arms and the inscription of the opening of the earlier bridge. Sadly this third bridge was unable to cope with modern volumes of traffic and was replaced in 1941 by the current structure, which is functional but far less attractive than its predecessor.

The first turf of the Deeside Extension Railway west of Banchory was cut on Friday 2 October 1857 at Rosehill, which lies about three quarters of a mile below the village of Charleston of Aboyne near the Loch of Aboyne. The first trains travelled on this extension on 2 December 1859, the journey from Aberdeen taking just over two hours. The following year the Royal Train carrying Queen Victoria took Her Majesty to Aboyne, from where she continued her journey to Balmoral by coach. This picture shows the railway track on the approach to Aboyne from the east in the late nineteenth century. The signal box, station buildings and extensive goods yard to the right of the station can be clearly identified.

An unusual view of Aboyne station as seen from the cab of one of the electric railcars which were introduced on the Deeside line in 1958. These railcars were powered by batteries which were recharged at Aberdeen and Ballater. It is said that the drivers never really trusted the Aberdeen staff to do the job properly and were always relieved to reach Ballater with some power left. In 1962 problems were experienced with the railcars and they were withdrawn, although in 1984 they were restored to working order and used on the privately-owned East Lancashire Railway north of Manchester. They are presently in a railway museum in the north of England, but attempts are being made to return them to Deeside where they would be used by the Royal Deeside Railway Preservation Society on a section of the old line east of Banchory which it is hoped will be restored shortly.

The original station buildings were somewhat less grand than the fine structure that was rebuilt on the site in the 1890s (shown on the right in this picture). Happily this building has survived, and has been tastefully converted into shops with a new housing development to the rear.

Station Square, Aboyne

The firm of John Troup, 'Purveyor of Meat', has occupied this site (also visible on the far left in the upper picture) since 1869 and this postcard, showing the owner and his staff in attendance, dates from the turn of the twentieth century. Note the man on the right in the uniform of a colour sergeant of a Scottish regiment who had in all probability just returned from fighting in the Boer War.

Aboyne Castle, which stands on a site just north of the village, is the residence of the Marquis of Huntly, 'Cock o' the North'. It has seen many changes over the years and bears little resemblance now to its appearance in this picture, which was taken during the First World War when it was used as a hospital for wounded servicemen. The oldest part of the building is the tower house which dates from the seventeenth century and was added to extensively in the nineteenth century. In recent years the Victorian additions have been removed, and some of the stonework used to restore the remaining tower house in seventeenth century Scottish castellated style.

The Marquis of Huntly and guests photographed at the annual Highland Games on Aboyne village green in the early years of the twentieth century. Apart from during the two World Wars, the Aboyne Games have been held annually since 1867. They traditionally took place on the first Wednesday of September but more recently the day has been changed to the first Saturday of August. In 1952 the committee of the games introduced the 'Aboyne dress' for women dancers. This was designed to replace the kilt and tunic and was essentially based on the costume of women in the eighteenth century.

Highland gatherings were certainly held on the green long before the Jacobite rising of 1745, and the organisers of the modern games have encouraged a revival of the traditions, symbolism and pageantry of earlier times in an attempt to recreate the historic clan meetings of the past. The games are always a popular event, as illustrated in this picture dating from the early days of the last century. The spire of the then United Free Church is prominent in the background, with the Huntly Arms Hotel to the left. In 1946 the church was sold to the Freemasons and is now the Temple of Lodge Charleston of Aboyne.

Leaving Aboyne on the North Deeside Road and turning right at the 31st milestone takes one to Tarland in the Howe of Cromar. The House of Cromar, now Alastrean House, stands in a beautiful setting and commands an extensive view of the Howe. It was formerly the home of the Marquis and Marchioness of Aberdeen and Temair, but in 1943 Lady MacRobert of Douneside generously placed the house at the disposal of the RAF as a 'Rest and Guest House'. It was renamed Alastrean House (Alastrean meaning 'Hearth of Honour for Winged Heroes of the Stars') and is now maintained by the MacRobert Trust.

ALASTREAN HOUSE, TARLAND.   A.7594.

The Square in Tarland, with its memorial to the fallen of both World Wars visible in the distance and the impressive MacRobert Memorial Hall to the left, has changed little over the last fifty years. The hall was erected in 1951 as a lasting memorial to Lady MacRobert's three sons, Alasdair, Roderic and Iain, who were all killed while serving with the RAF. To the right, just in the picture, is the end of the Aberdeen Arms, the local hotel and a reminder of the earlier laird, the Marquis of Aberdeen.

THE SQUARE, TARLAND   D 3195

The road from Tarland towards Loch Kinord and Cambus O' May leads to Lochhead, once a popular stopping place for tourists. The garden there contained a unique clock driven by water-power, which was removed prior to Word War II. Nearby is the Burn o' Vat, one of the most popular picnic spots on Deeside. Many tales of outlaws and smugglers centre around the vat, which made an ideal hide-out and is often wrongly referred to as Rob Roy's cave. It is more likely that it was used by Gilderoy, a notorious outlaw who made frequent raids in the area. He was finally brought to justice and publicly hanged in Edinburgh in 1636.

BALLATER, CAMBUS O MAY STATION

Cambus O' May station was perched on a narrow shelf overlooking the river. In the early 1900s the directors of the Great North of Scotland Railway occasionally held board meetings in a coach which was shunted into the siding which adjoined the main line here. This meant that they could conduct their business and at the same time look out on one of the loveliest views on Deeside. The name Cambus O' May has Gaelic origins and means 'bend in the plain', which well describes the double bend in the river with flat ground to the east and west. Special deliveries of explosives were once made to the station for use in the nearby quarry.

Dating from 1905, this suspension bridge was partly funded by the railway company and provided access to Cambus O' May station from the south side of the river. With the closure of the line it fell into disrepair and in 1988 was replaced by a new bridge, which was opened by Her Majesty Queen Elizabeth, the Queen Mother. Unlike its predecessor, the new bridge does not span the old railway line.

Returning to Aboyne and taking the South Deeside Road westwards, one arrives at the Tower of Ess and a road leading into the Glentanar Estate. In 1869 William Cunliffe Brooks, a wealthy Manchester banker who was later knighted, arrived at Glen Tanar (also spelt Tanner or Tana) as a tenant of the Marquis of Huntly. Between the years 1888 and 1899 he acquired large estates on Deeside including Aboyne and Glentanar and left his indelible mark in the form of the architecture of those estates. Fenton Wyness, the prominent historian and architect, summed up Sir Cunliffe's achievements thus: 'it is clear that he failed to appreciate that Scotland possessed any architectural tradition for he immediately set about eliminating everything which appeared incongruous to his English eyes.' Following his death the estate was bought by George Coats of the Paisley cotton firm in 1905; he was created 1st Baron Glentanar in 1916. The house has been substantially modified in recent years and is now owned by the Hon. Jean Bruce, granddaughter of the first baron.

Glentanar House, Aboyne.

In 1870 Cunliffe Brooks began building the beautiful Episcopal chapel of St Lesmo. It originally had heather thatching, but this has since been replaced by slates and an open-timbered wooden roof. The pews are lined with deerskin and the altar is formed from a great stone found in the bed of the Tanar. On his death in 1900 the laird was buried in the burial ground beside the church. St Lesmo's Well, which is inscribed 'Drink, Weary Pilgrim, Drink and Pray', is nearby. St Lesmo is claimed to have brought Christianity to this neighbourhood in the eighth century.

The youthful George Gordon, later 6th Lord Byron (1788–1824), spent some time at the farm of Ballaterach (pronounced Ballatrich) during the summers of 1795–1797 whilst a student at Aberdeen Grammar School. At the time the farm was tenanted by James Robertson. Byron's affection for Deeside is well-known through his works. Mary Robertson, a daughter of the farmer, was one of his companions and is the heroine of his poem *When I Roved a Young Highlander*. During the summer of 1803 when he was a pupil at Harrow he returned to Deeside and climbed Lochnagar. Later in life he wrote about the mountain in expressive terms:

England! thy beauties are tame and domestic

To one who has roved o'er the mountains afar;   The steep frowning glories of dark Lochnagar!
Oh for the crags that are wild and majestic!

Pannanich Wells, with its hotel, is just under two miles from Ballater on the South Deeside Road. It is said that the wells began to attract attention some time in the mid-eighteenth century when an old woman, Elspet or Isabella Michie, who suffered from scrofula (a form of tuberculosis sometimes known as the 'King's Evil'), bathed in the muddy pools and drank the spa waters. Gradually the old woman's health improved, and as news of the miracle cure spread Colonel Francis Farquharson of Monaltrie, called 'Baron Ban' because of his fair hair, had the water analysed. Becoming convinced of its medicinal properties, he had the wells cleaned out and built an inn for those who flocked to the area to test the waters for themselves. Soon the accommodation could not cope with the influx, and nearby Ballater was developed by the colonel's nephew and successor William Farquharson. The water from the wells is now being bottled and sold, but its advocates claim no miraculous powers for it, stating only that it appears good for the health.

Ballater from South-East

The story of the bridge over the Dee at Ballater is told on a plaque on the west parapet. 'A bridge of stone was built about 100 yards east of this site in 1783 and was swept away by flood in 1799. A second bridge of stone was built by Telford 60 feet east of this site in 1809 and was swept away by floods in 1829. It was replaced by a wooden bridge in 1834 which lasted till 6 Nov. 1885, when this bridge, built by County Road Trustees, was opened by HM Queen Victoria who named it the Royal Bridge. Long may it stand.' The restored plaque was unveiled by Queen Elizabeth on 8 September 1998. Also visible in the picture is the Invercauld Arms Hotel (which has now reverted to its original name, the Monaltrie Hotel), with its mock-Tudor extension on the riverside, and Glenmuick Church in the Square which dates from 1873.

BRIDGE STREET, BALLATER.

Ballater is a comparatively modern village, dating from around 1798, its name coming from the Gaelic *baille challater* meaning 'town of the wooded stream'. It owes its origins to the popularity of the Pannanich Wells and the need to develop accommodation for the many visitors who came to the area looking for cures. The building on the right dates from 1906 and when this picture was taken the corner shop was occupied by Knowles the jeweller with James Strachan, butcher, next door. The latter shop was originally home to the Victoria tearooms with the Victoria Boarding House above. The well-known journalist Cuthbert Graham described the town as follows: 'Ballater is on a checkerboard plan. Its main thoroughfare Bridge Street, lined with shops, many of which display the insignia to which royal warrant holders are entitled, runs north from the bridge to the Station Square and is intersected half way along by The Square, a wide and long village green, on which the only building is the stately Glenmuick Church.' Many of the shops in Bridge Street proudly display the insignia of royal warrant-holders, granted by the Queen, Prince of Wales and the Queen Mother.

The Station Square in Ballater in the early 1900s with the wooden station buildings on the left, and on the right the solid granite buildings given to the people of Ballater by Alexander Gordon, a wealthy brewer of London and native of Glenmuick. The central portion set back from the road is known as the Gordon Institute. The Albert Memorial Hall, bearing the inscription 'A Prince Indeed. Above all titles a Household Word', is the substantial building in the middle distance on the right. After the railway line reached Ballater in 1866 the town became the arrival point for members of the royal family en route to Balmoral Castle. Had the line continued to Braemar as originally intended, Ballater's development as a tourist centre might not have been so spectacular. Work on continuing the line beyond Ballater was actually started, but the project was halted by Queen Victoria who did not want a railway passing near her estate.

In 1923, with the formation of the 'big four' railway companies, the Great North of Scotland Railway became the Northern Scottish area of the London and North Eastern Railway. This Thornycroft 20-seater bus was new in 1926 and operated the Braemar–Balmoral–Ballater service. It is seen here at Ballater railway station. Alexander of Falkirk took over operations in 1930 and the bus became part of their well-known blue-liveried fleet.

It is inevitable that some reference must be made to John Brown, Queen Victoria's personal attendant, in a book on Deeside. Born at Crathienaird near Balmoral on 28 December 1827, Brown was the second son of a farmer who had also been a schoolteacher. When he was five the family moved to Bush Farm (this picture shows the farmhouse kitchen there). John Brown began work at the age of thirteen, and in 1849 became one of the Balmoral ghillies. He was in very frequent attendance on the Queen, and in 1851 permanently entered the Royal Service, gradually rising through the ranks through good conduct and intelligence. In 1858 he was appointed the Queen's Personal Servant in Scotland, and in February 1865 this appointment was extended to wherever Her Majesty may be. Brown was promoted to become an upper servant in December of the same year. In March 1872 the Queen conferred her gold Victoria Devoted Service medal upon John Brown in recognition of his presence of mind on the occasion of the attack made by Arthur O'Connor upon Her Majesty in Buckingham Palace Gardens. On his death in 1883 a grateful Queen erected a statue of Brown in the grounds of Balmoral. The statue was later moved and can now be seen in the woods to the south of the old dairy.

Birkhall was built by the Gordons of Abergeldie in 1715. In 1849 it was purchased by Queen Victoria for the Prince of Wales but he only used it once – in 1862 – preferring Abergeldie Castle. Since then it has been used regularly by members of the royal family. Most recently Queen Elizabeth, the Queen Mother has used it as her holiday home on her visits to Deeside.

BIRKHALL, BALLATER

Abergeldie Castle and Bridge.

Abergeldie Castle lies six miles from Ballater on the south bank of the Dee and its estate adjoins that of Balmoral. The original building was a plain, square-turreted tower dating from the sixteenth century, but after the estate was leased by Queen Victoria considerable additions were made and the house was made more comfortable for the reception of guests. It was frequently occupied by Queen Victoria's mother, the Duchess of Kent, until her death in 1861; thereafter it was used by the Prince of Wales (the future King Edward VII) and his family. The adjoining Georgian mansion has now been demolished. The suspension footbridge which links the castle with the north bank of the Dee was built in 1885 and replaced a rope and cradle bridge which had been one of the 'sights' of Deeside.

THE CHANCEL, CRATHIE CHURCH, BALMORAL.

The present Crathie Church stands on the site of the original 1804 building. Queen Victoria regularly worshipped at the old church on her visits to Balmoral between 1848 and the building of the present church, which she laid the foundation stone of on 11 September 1893. It was dedicated on 19 June 1895. Succeeding sovereigns have regularly worshipped in the church throughout the years of their reigns, and the royal family have presented many of its furnishings and beautified it with memorials. The hexagonal pulpit incorporates no less than eighteen varieties of Scottish granite and the communion table is carved from Iona marble. The baptismal font is made of polished granite from the Kemnay and Rubislaw (Aberdeen) quarries. The bust of Queen Victoria is set immediately above the foundation stone she laid.

Their Majesties King George V and Queen Mary return to Balmoral having attended the weekly service at Crathie Church.

The Glen Muick road follows the river to the Linn of Muick. The river runs through a rocky gorge with a waterfall that is especially fine when the Linn is in spate. The road continues up the glen and terminates at the Spital, where the Capel Mounth Pass across the Grampians begins. Beyond the Spital is Loch Muick with the great mountains rising steeply from its shores.

The magnificent mass of Lochnagar may not be the highest of Scottish mountains, but it is Deeside's mountain. It dominates the scenery for miles around and takes its name from the small loch beneath its northern precipice called Lochnagar, or the Goat's Loch.

Invercauld House, Braemar

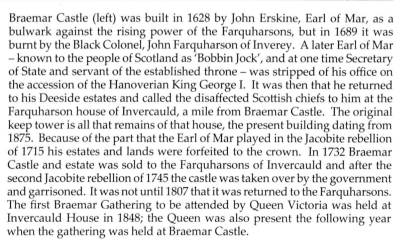

Braemar Castle (left) was built in 1628 by John Erskine, Earl of Mar, as a bulwark against the rising power of the Farquharsons, but in 1689 it was burnt by the Black Colonel, John Farquharson of Inverey. A later Earl of Mar – known to the people of Scotland as 'Bobbin Jock', and at one time Secretary of State and servant of the established throne – was stripped of his office on the accession of the Hanoverian King George I. It was then that he returned to his Deeside estates and called the disaffected Scottish chiefs to him at the Farquharson house of Invercauld, a mile from Braemar Castle. The original keep tower is all that remains of that house, the present building dating from 1875. Because of the part that the Earl of Mar played in the Jacobite rebellion of 1715 his estates and lands were forfeited to the crown. In 1732 Braemar Castle and estate was sold to the Farquharsons of Invercauld and after the second Jacobite rebellion of 1745 the castle was taken over by the government and garrisoned. It was not until 1807 that it was returned to the Farquharsons. The first Braemar Gathering to be attended by Queen Victoria was held at Invercauld House in 1848; the Queen was also present the following year when the gathering was held at Braemar Castle.

Braemar im Winter
Invercauld Arms Hotel

In Scottish history, Braemar is noted for the part it played in the Jacobite rising of 1715. The first building reached on entering the village is the Invercauld Arms, and it was on that very site that the standard which marked the start of the Jacobite rebellion of 1715 was raised. Opposite the hotel is a cairn 'erected by the Deeside Field Club in 1953 [the] Coronation year of Elizabeth Queen of Scots to commemorate the raising of the standard on 6th September, 1715 by John Erskine, Earl of Mar. A tablet in the Invercauld Arms Hotel marks the spot where the standard was raised. Add Glory to the Past' (the brass tablet can be seen in the lounge of the hotel). The risings of both 1715 and 1745 were dismal failures, and the local Jacobites suffered for their loyalty.

Curling is a game of Scottish origin now played in many other parts of the world. Here a match (bonspiel) is in progress, probably on Aboyne Loch, although the card claims it to be Braemar. Modern curlers will find most of the detail familiar: the stones, brushes (besoms) and sweeping. A curler is throwing his stone using the footboard (crampit) to save him falling flat on his face when delivering his stone. When conditions were right for curling at Aboyne, the Great North of Scotland Railway Company used to lay on special trains from Aberdeen, stopping at the temporary platform which was used between 1888 and 1930 for excursions in the summer and bonspiels in the winter.

Fife Arms Hotel Braemar

Braemar stands on the banks of the Clunie Water and really consists of two villages – Castleton, which is the older of the two, on the east bank, and Auchindryne on the opposite bank. This photograph shows the Fife Arms Hotel, probably on games day, with the crowds heading to the park. The bridge over the Clunie in the background was erected in 1863 to link the two villages. In the distance is the tower of the Scottish Episcopalian Church of St Margaret. It is most appropriate that the flag of St Andrew should fly from the tower because it was to Braemar that the hallowed relics of the saint were brought and venerated by the Pictish King Angus some time in the middle of the eighth century.

Seen here in the early 1950s is AV 8323, an Albion with a Cowieson body that belonged to the Deeside Omnibus Service operated by Mrs Helen Strachan of Ballater. It is depicted here as No. 24, although it was originally No. 13. The vehicle's bodywork was rebuilt by Walker of Aberdeen after the Second World War. The conductress has been identified as Nancy McIntosh who is delivering a parcel to Andrew Collie's shop. Collie's main shop stood on the corner of Union Street and Bon Accord Street in Aberdeen, and generations of Aberdonians will recall the aroma of roasted coffee beans as they passed by it.

MAIN STREET. BRAEMAR.

Braemar can experience a relatively wide range of temperatures and snow scenes such as the one on page 42 are not uncommon. Local highs and lows are faithfully recorded in the observatory situated close to the hotel which was established by the Prince Consort in 1855. On 11 February 1895 – and more recently on 10 January 1982 – the temperature fell to -27 °C, the lowest temperature ever to be recorded in the United Kingdom. Braemar can enjoy excellent summer weather, however, which has meant that it has been a popular holiday resort for some time. In more recent years it has been a busy ski centre in winter, as well as providing a gateway to some of the finest mountain country in Scotland.

The private Victoria Bridge over the Dee lies over three miles west of Braemar and provides access to Mar Lodge. The lodge illustrated here was the creation of Princess Louise, the Princess Royal, eldest daughter of Edward VII. It was not, however, the first Mar Lodge, which was bought by the Earl of Fife in the eighteenth century and stood behind the present building. In the middle of the following century the family built a new mansion on the south side of the Dee which they first called Corriemulzie Cottage and later New Mar Lodge. This was destroyed by fire in 1885. The sixth Earl of Fife married Princess Louise in 1889 and was created Duke of Fife in 1900. Queen Victoria laid the foundation stone of the Mar Lodge pictured here in 1895 and the building was completed in 1898. It was later sold and became a hotel. Today the lodge and estate are managed by The National Trust for Scotland.

Six miles from Braemar the road reaches the Linn o' Dee. The bridge over the Linn was built in 1857 by James, Earl of Fife and opened by Queen Victoria. It replaced an earlier structure described as an 'auld, rickety, widden brig' that was carried away in the great flood of 1829. The Linn is a picturesque spot at the termination of the Deeside road which is much frequented by visitors.

- The Cottage, Braemar. -
(Here R.L.Stevenson spent the summer
of 1881 and wrote "Treasure Island"
his first great work.)

In the summer of 1881 Robert Louis Stevenson spent seven weeks in Braemar, accompanied by his parents, his wife and her 13 year old son Lloyd Osbourne. The cottage that they stayed in had been owned by Miss Mary Macgregor who had died in 1880. In a letter from Braemar RLS wrote 'The rain rains and the winds beat upon the cottage of the late Miss Macgregor', although despite the bad weather the holiday did the author much good. It was while in Braemar that he wrote *Treasure Island*. The story grew out of a map painted by young Lloyd Osbourne who suggested to his stepfather that he write a story round it. Stevenson did so, and after dinner each evening read what he had written that day. In this way the fascinating tale came into being on Deeside, far from the scene of the narrative. The cottage can still be seen in Castleton Terrace, just beyond the Scottish Episcopalian Church of St Margaret.

THE DEVIL'S ELBOW (THE HIGHEST PUBLIC ROAD IN GREAT BRITAIN, 2199 FT. ABOVE SEA LEVEL).

R. 217504. J.V.

On leaving Braemar and travelling south, the Cairnwell road initially follows the line of the Clunie Water. It becomes the highest public road in the country, however, and as it gains altitude the scenery becomes very desolate. Originally it would have been little used in the winter months, but with the great upsurge in skiing and the building of ski lifts and tows at the road's highest point (2,199 feet), it is kept clear to allow thousands of people to reach the slopes. The famous 'Devil's Elbow', a double bend which at one time had to be negotiated with extreme care, was on the other side of the summit. The road has now been straightened and the bend totally eliminated. The bus belonged to the General Omnibus Company of London and was photographed in the 1930s.